HOW TO DRAW AND COLOUR STEAMPUNK MACHINES

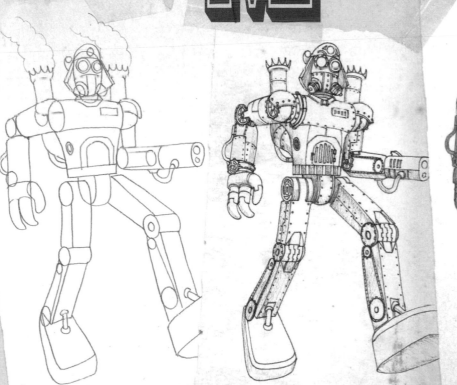

MARK BERGIN

Published in Great Britain in MMXIV by
Book House, an imprint of
The Salariya Book Company Ltd
25 Marlborough Place, Brighton BN1 1UB
www.salariya.com
www.book-house.co.uk

PB ISBN-13: 978-1-908973-73-3

Editor: Victoria England

1 3 5 7 9 8 6 4 2

A CIP catalogue record for this book is available
from the British Library.

Printed and bound in China.

Visit
www.salariya.com
for our online catalogue and
free interactive web books.

PAPER FROM
SUSTAINABLE
FORESTS

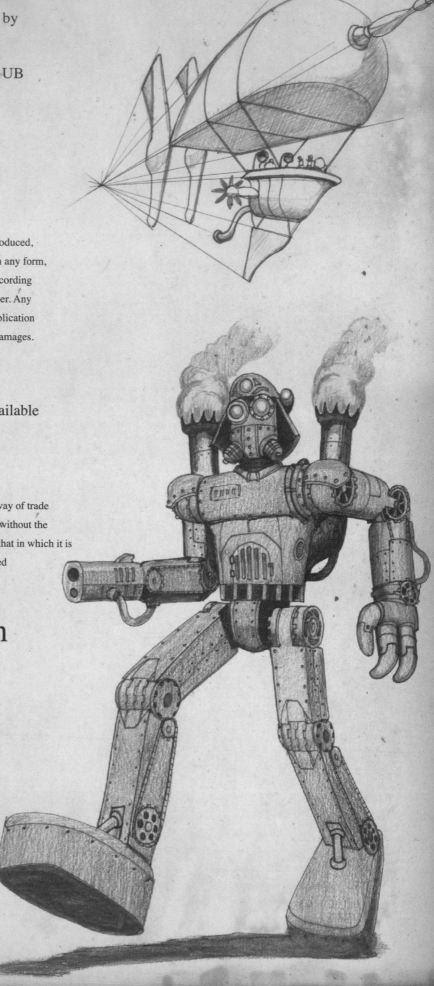

CONTENTS

INTRODUCTION

Dirigible
Balloon

Steam Bike

Steampunk is a popular artistic movement that spans many genres. The inspiration for this form of Victorian futurism, with its sepia-tinted world of havoc-wreaking machines and fantasy gadgetry, was originally born from the masters of science-fiction literature.

You can start an artistic adventure and use this book as your secret weapon to learn how to draw and colour your own gargantuan Steampunk creations.

Massive machines are integral to the Steampunk world, from gigantic Dirigible Balloons to Aquatilus Submarines. Create the unimaginable using a variety of drawing and colouring methods and tools. This book will provide you with step-by-step guides and handy tips, as well as the knowledge and enthusiasm to launch your own Steampunk universe.

Steam Robot

Speedster

Flying Bug Bike

DRAWING TOOLS

Learn about the many tools and materials that you can use to translate your inventive speculations onto paper. You do not need lots of equipment – the basic pencil is the most versatile tool. Explore different ways of making marks to discover your own style.

Steam Bike

Ink pens are ideal for sketching. Develop different tones by building up layers of shading.

Tone

Using tone makes your drawings look more real and 3D. The darkest areas of your drawing can be inked in solidly but leave the lightest areas ink-free. Use cross-hatching for darker tones and hatching for midtones (see below).

Cross-hatching   Hatching

Felt-tips are great for filling in areas of flat tone.

Dramatic use of light is called chiaroscuro – an Italian word for 'light–dark'.

Steam Tractor

Steam Planes

Pencils

Pencils come in different grades of hardness and each creates a different type of line, from fine greys to soft fluffy blacks.

Hard pencils are graded from H to 6H (the hardest). Soft pencils are graded from B to 9B (the softest and blackest).

HB pencils are ideal for general sketching. But try experimenting with different grades of pencils to achieve a variety of tonal effects.

Draughtsmen's pens

Draughtsmen's pens and art pens are ideal for creating fine, regular lines and surface texture. A variety of pen nib widths are available.

Submarine

Try out new approaches by experimenting with drawing papers. They are available in various surface textures from smooth to very rough. Rough paper is ideal for use with charcoal, whereas smooth paper is best for fine line drawings.

7

IDEAS

Steampunk is an artistic movement with endless creative possibilities. Its roots are in the Industrial Revolution: an era of great change, from manufacturing techniques to transport, offering plenty of new technology from which to draw inspiration. Be inspired by lost items from the gaslit past and use old photographs to let your imagination run full steam ahead!

Machinery

Steampunk art draws heavily on Victorian machinery. Cogs, wheels and rivets appear in abundance. Try searching through second-hand shops for old-fashioned mechanisms or watches to whet your Steampunk appetite.

Reinventing equipment

Modern equipment can be reincarnated in a fictional Victorian age. Imagine your digital equipment and techno mechanisms driven by steam and clockwork!

Inspiration

Let the Industrial Revolution ignite your artistic speculation. Victorian transport included the steam train, horse and cart, steamboats and sometimes even cars. Why not visit a steam rally for inspiration?

Instruments

Dream in brass. Take inspiration from unlikely items such as musical instruments or veteran cars.

Decoration

Steampunk blurs the line between tool and decoration. It is a design aesthetic that values detail, detail and more detail! Think brass and copper, glass and polished wood, engraving and etching.

Inventions

The Victorian and Edwardian eras, while filled with traditional values, were a playground for invention and discovery. Take inspiration from inventions like the lightbulb and dream up your own zany mechanical miracles.

PERSPECTIVE I

In one-point perspective, lines converge at a single V.P. You can change the position of the V.P. to adjust the viewer's eye-level.

V.P.

Bring your creations to life! Drawing in perspective creates a 3D illusion of space, speed and depth in your sketchbook. The vanishing point (V.P.) is where receding parallel lines appear to meet. By changing the height of the V.P. you can give your locomotives, submarines and airships added drama.

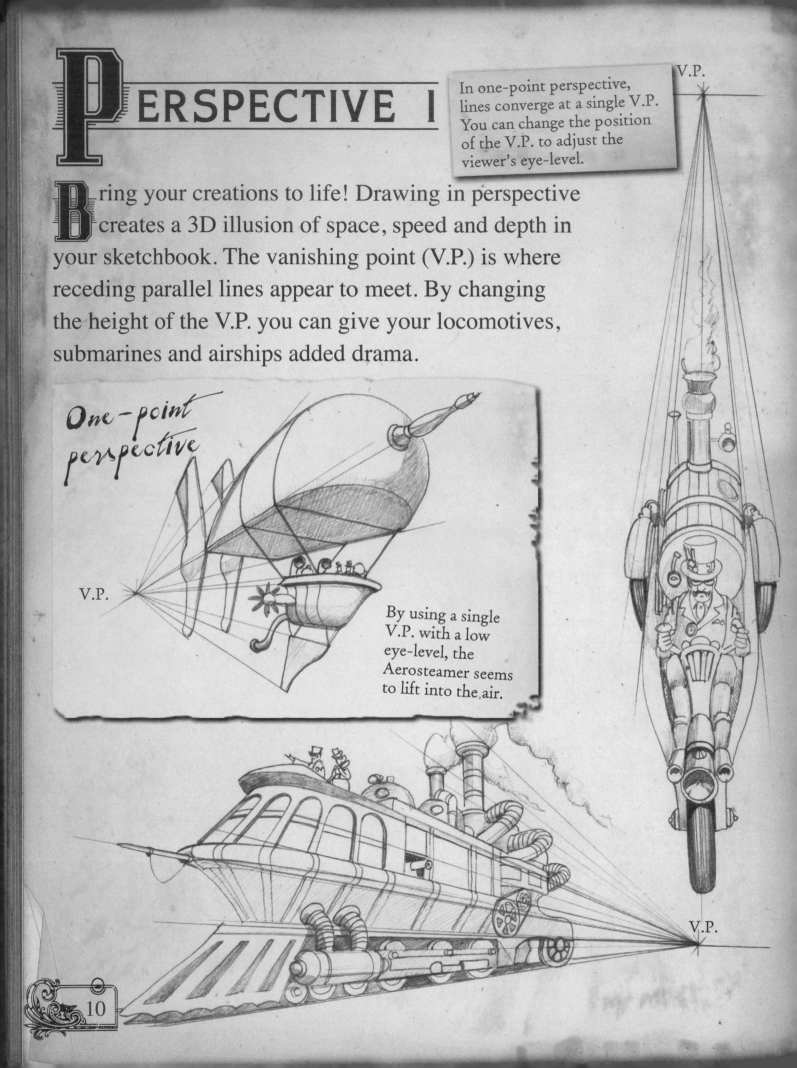

One-point perspective

V.P.

By using a single V.P. with a low eye-level, the Aerosteamer seems to lift into the air.

V.P.

V.P.

10

Normal eye-level

V.P. is on the horizon.

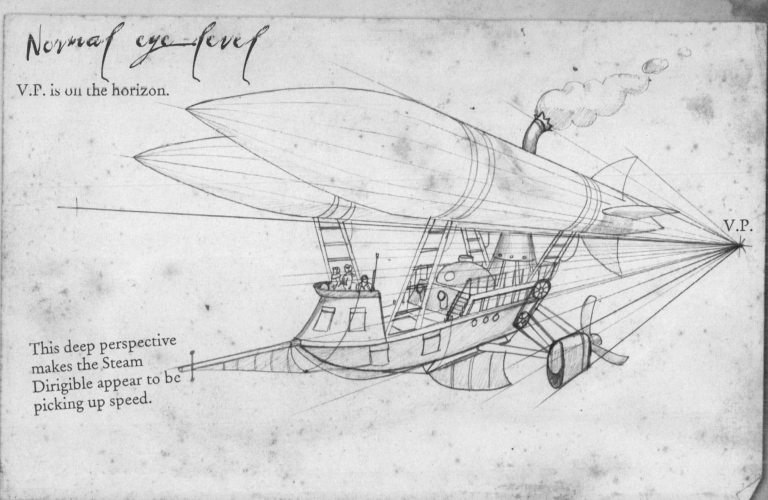

V.P.

This deep perspective makes the Steam Dirigible appear to be picking up speed.

Two-point perspective

By using two-point perspective you can create realistic drawings that jump straight out from your sketchbook.

The high V.P. suggests that we are looking down at the craft from above.

V.P.

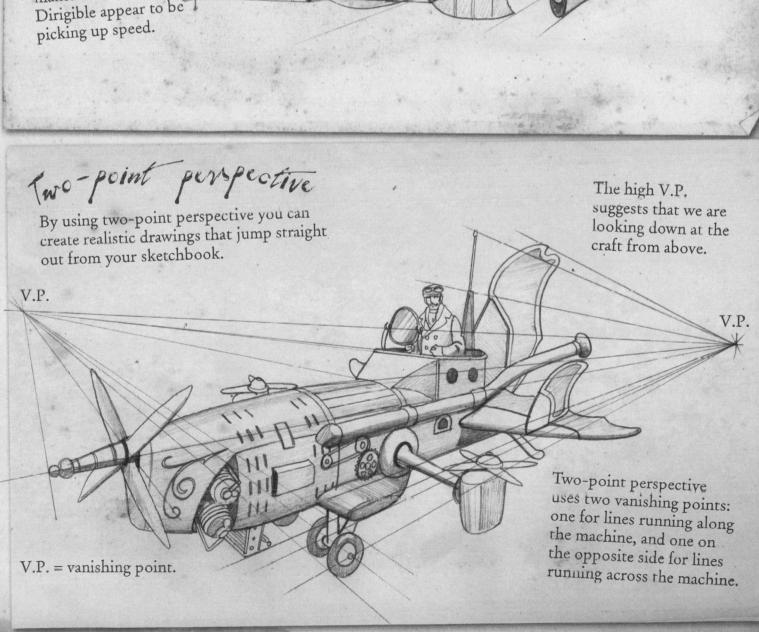

V.P.

Two-point perspective uses two vanishing points: one for lines running along the machine, and one on the opposite side for lines running across the machine.

V.P. = vanishing point.

PERSPECTIVE 2

Two- and-three point perspective makes your drawings even more realistic and creates dramatic viewpoints. Having an idea of the viewer's eye level is helpful so you can apply the right perspective guidelines.

V.P.

This three-point perspective drawing uses a V.P. for converging lines that run along the machine, and another V.P. on the opposite side for lines running across it. The third V.P. is above.

Three-point perspective

Three-point perspective is used when the chosen viewpoint is either very low or very high.

Drawing Automaton-Gargantuan from an extremely low eye-level makes it look huge and dominating.

V.P.

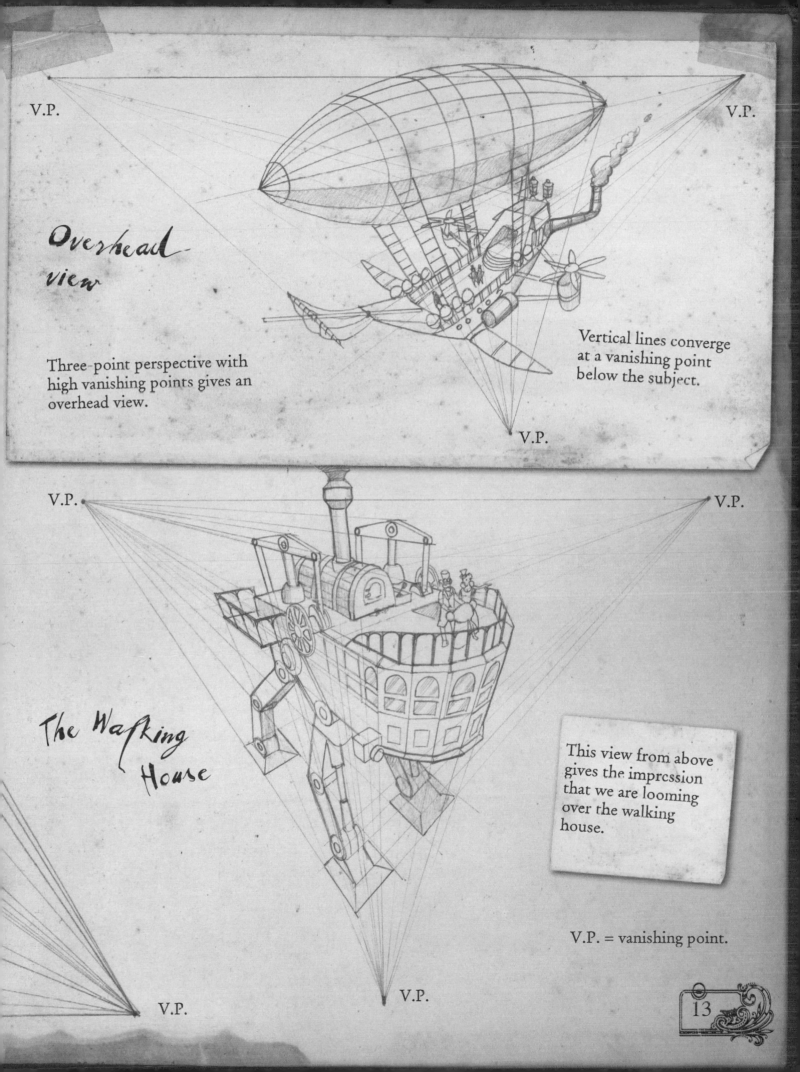

Overhead view

Three-point perspective with high vanishing points gives an overhead view.

Vertical lines converge at a vanishing point below the subject.

V.P.

V.P.

V.P.

The Walking House

This view from above gives the impression that we are looming over the walking house.

V.P. = vanishing point.

V.P.

V.P.

COLOUR

Enhance your drawing by introducing your Steampunk machines to a world of colour. Learn how to use these essential techniques to ignite the black and white past into a technicolor futurism.

Watercolour paints are ideal for creating a luminous finish, perfect for all your brass and copper fixtures. Apply thin washes (translucent coats of colour) to your drawings.

Watercolour paints

Water-soluble pencils

Water-soluble pencils offer a versatile combination of drawing and painting. You can create lines or colour washes by adding water to parts of your drawing.

Why not try to build
up different textures,
layers and hues?
Experimenting with
colour will bring your
parallel world to life.

Ink wash

This effect is achieved by
completing your drawing in
ink lines and then sweeping
light strokes of diluted ink
over your drawing.

Coloured pencils

Coloured pencils are ideal
for adding crisp details to
your drawing, and work
well in combination with
coloured inks. The leads
are usually fairly soft and
easily blended.

DESIGN YOUR OWN

Steampunk is all about asking yourself 'what if?' Let your dreams and desires inspire these machines, and your drawings will bring them to life. Design your Steampunk machines with your unique mix of alternative gadgetry and bygone paraphernalia. But don't forget the most important rule: have fun!

Will your machine soar through the sky or race beneath the waves? Perhaps it might be driven through the foggy, gaslit streets of a Dickensian metropolis.

Form and Function

Function is as important as form. How will your captain fit inside?

Features

Become a Steampunk tinkerer: work out which features and functions will make your machine unique and incorporate them into your design.

Accessories

Added features such as detachable pods containing important items and extendable arms can truly make your creation your own.

TURBOUNUS MOTORBIKE

The Turbounus Motorbike is the fastest form of aerodynamic transport for a lone rider. It is fitted with a vaporising mechanism to dissolve attackers in pursuit while it travels at breakneck speed. It is armoured with robust, shiny steel.

1 Roughly sketch the outline of the motorbike using an HB pencil.

2 Use curved lines to sketch in larger details such as the windshield, handlebars and driver's seat.

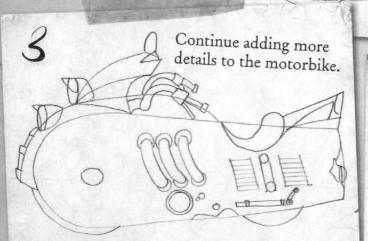

3 Continue adding more details to the motorbike.

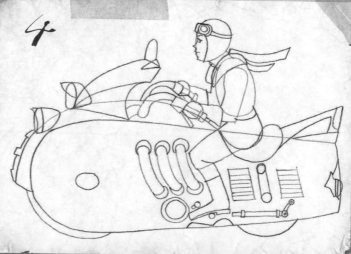

4

Add the rider in her Steampunk attire. Don't forget her iconic brass goggles!

18

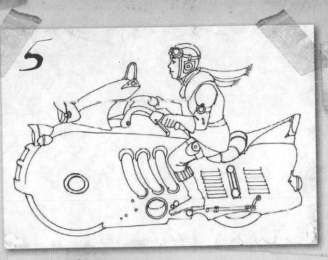

5

Now the basic structure is in place, begin building up the finer details

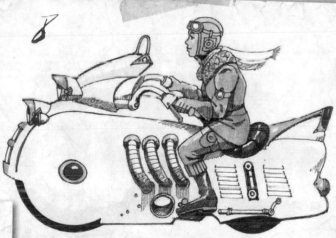

6

Switch to a softer pencil and go over the original sketch to define the lines clearly. Add shading to create shadows and depth.

7

Experiment with different colour schemes until you find the perfect mood. Start adding colour to the larger parts of the drawing first.

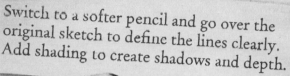

Now apply colour to the finer details.

8

Add decorative details of your own. Put in a shadow beneath the bike to make it look truly three-dimensional.

9

FLYING BUG BIKE

Adorned with brass fixtures and metallic embellishments, the Flying Bug Bike is elegantly crafted for an exquisite flight. This steam-powered creature's antenna can track incoming computer signals. It morphs into a bike by hatching wheels as it approaches the ground.

1

Lightly sketch in the Flying Bug's body using rounded shapes.

2

Establish a rough outline of the legs and wheels.

3

Continue to build up more detail. Draw as many extra fixtures and features as you desire.

4

Sketch in a basic outline of the driver, his controls and some of the bike's finer details.

Add shadows using a brown pencil. Sharpen the drawing by going over the lines to add definition.

5

6

Create shading and tone using watercolour paint.

7

Begin to add colour to the Bug, starting with the larger parts of the drawing first.

8

Now apply colour to the finer details. Use a bluish tone to shade areas that face away from the light.

9

Alternatively, why not use darker, sepia-toned colours to give your drawing a faded, antique look?

EMBERATRON GIANT

The Emberatron Giant, at 20 ft (6 m) in height, towers over all other machines. With his flame-throwing shoulder turrets, electric shotgun and solid steel armour, he can withstand the most vigorous lightning gun attacks.

Lightly sketch in simple shapes to build up the giant's body.

2

The right foot, because it is close to us, looms menacingly large. This is a good example of how perspective can make a drawing more dramatic.

3

4

Now sketch in the other limbs using cylinder-like shapes.

Continue refining the giant's features by adding more detail.

5

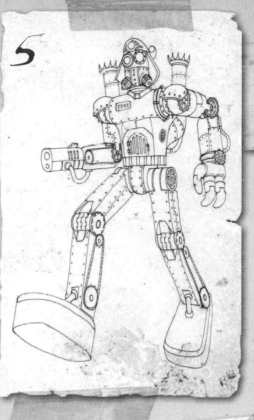

Add all the finer details and draw them in with an ink pen. Begin to add light and shade.

6

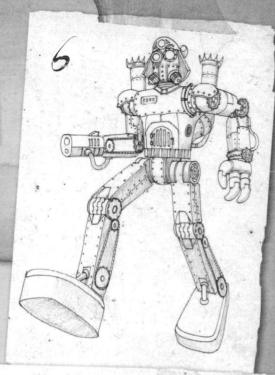

Using a coloured pencil, begin to add tone to the giant.

7

Choose a pencil of a similar colour and add another layer of tone.

Finally, strengthen the shadows and use different coloured pencils to add the glowing fires.

8

Hunting Machine

Captain Cuthbert's Hunting Machine with its mix of cogs, gears and steam power elevates its driver and removes him from all danger. Equipped with gaslit headlights, polished wooden exterior and built-in rifles, it can be identified by the wheezing noises that come from its pneumatic legs with each step.

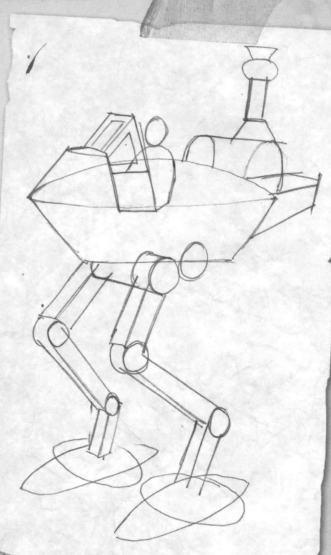

Establish the basic shapes with simple pencil lines and circles.

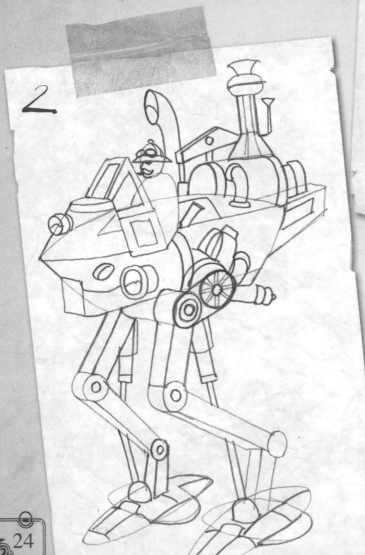

Draw in the machine's unique features such as the steam funnel, wheels, headlights and pipes.

3

Add further intricate details and create strong, well-defined lines by going over your pencil lines with ink.

Erase all your pencil construction lines.

4 Ink washes

Add ink washes to your drawing to create tone and shadow.

Add movement lines.

Wait for it to dry, then add the final precise details such as the rivets and the knots in the wood.

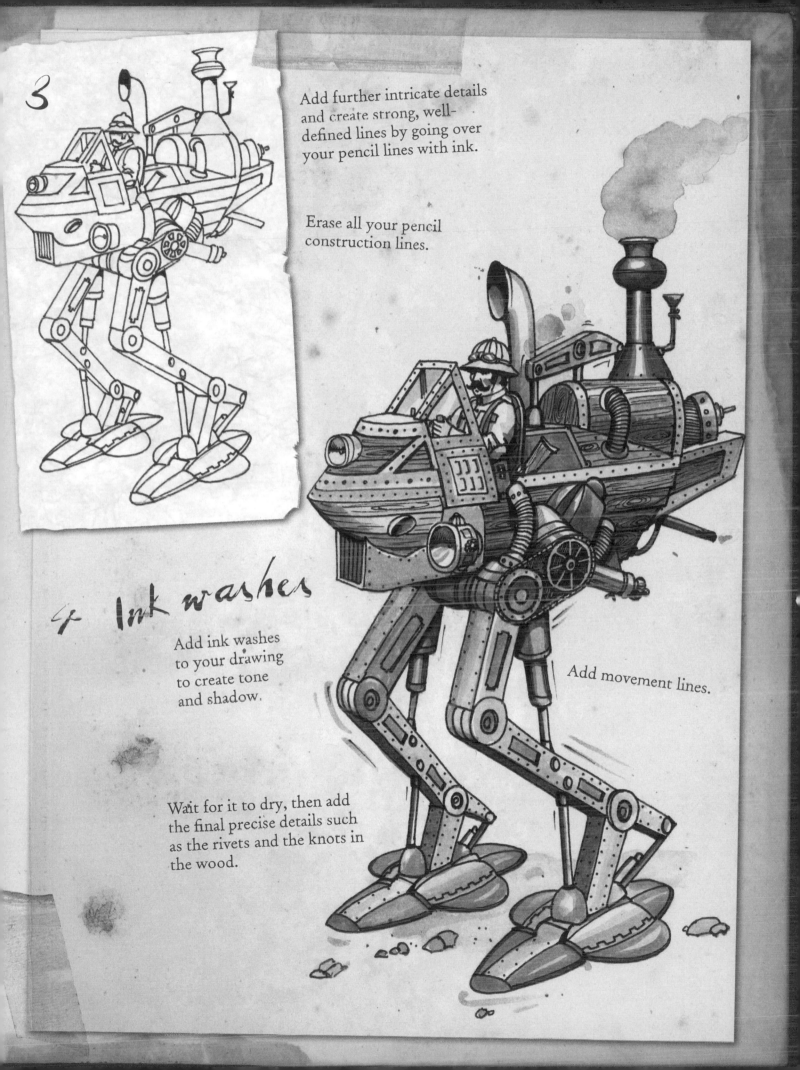

FLYING GALLEON

*G*liding through the clouds, the electric-propelled Flying Galleon defies gravity. Some see its crew as swashbuckling heroes, others as lawless marauders.

1 Use simple pencil lines to establish the ship's outline.

2 Add more detail.

3 Add the main outer features of the hull of the Galleon.

4 Add the engines and the front and rear propellers.

5

Draw in the remaining features: mast, sails, hot-air balloons and rigging.

6

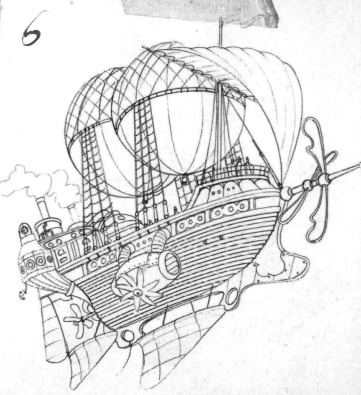

Add the final intricate details using pencil. Use very precise lines to achieve the right mechanical look.

7

Colouring

Complete the drawing by adding colour. Use watercolour washes to build up tone.

DIRIGIBLE BALLOON

Navigate the skies in comfort and style with your very own Dirigible Balloon. Its five-star living quarters make it the cream of the crop of elegant sky travel. Steam-driven propellers rotate at a gentle speed to ensure a smooth, comfortable journey through the sky.

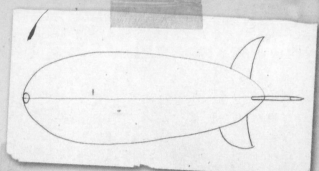

Lightly sketch in the rough shapes of the balloon and fins.

Add the cabin and engine room, above and below.

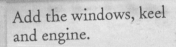

Add the windows, keel and engine.

Now refine all other details and create a sense of volume by drawing in curved lines along the body of the balloon.

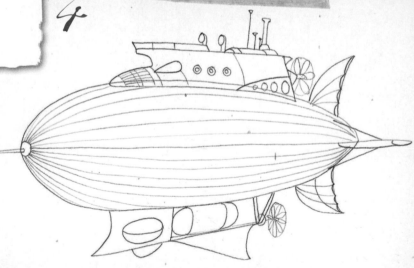

5

Add the craft's ID number. Tighten up the drawing with crisp lines. Add some shading to the underside of the balloon to create the illusion that the light is coming from above.

Use a light acrylic wash to colour in the balloon. Apply a stronger tone of acrylic paint to darker features. Add a further wash to the background.

6

7

Fine-tune and finish off all intricate details. Touches of darker paint will create a dramatic result.

Finish off by highlighting small areas of detail with a contrasting colour.

8

QUATILUS SUBMARINE

Explore the depths of the ocean with the Aquatilus Submarine. Made from solid steel, it sports a sharp ramming blade on its hull to capsize enemy ships.

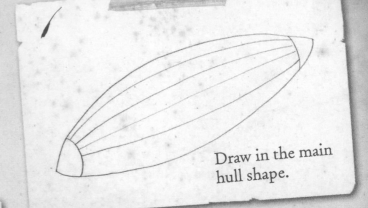

Draw in the main hull shape.

Add the superstructure and ballast tanks to the hull.

Add the controlling tail fins and rudder to the stern of the submarine.

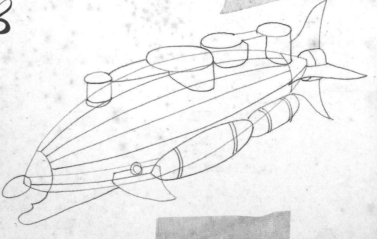

Draw in the remaining details: portholes, pipes, mechanics and of course the large ramming blade!

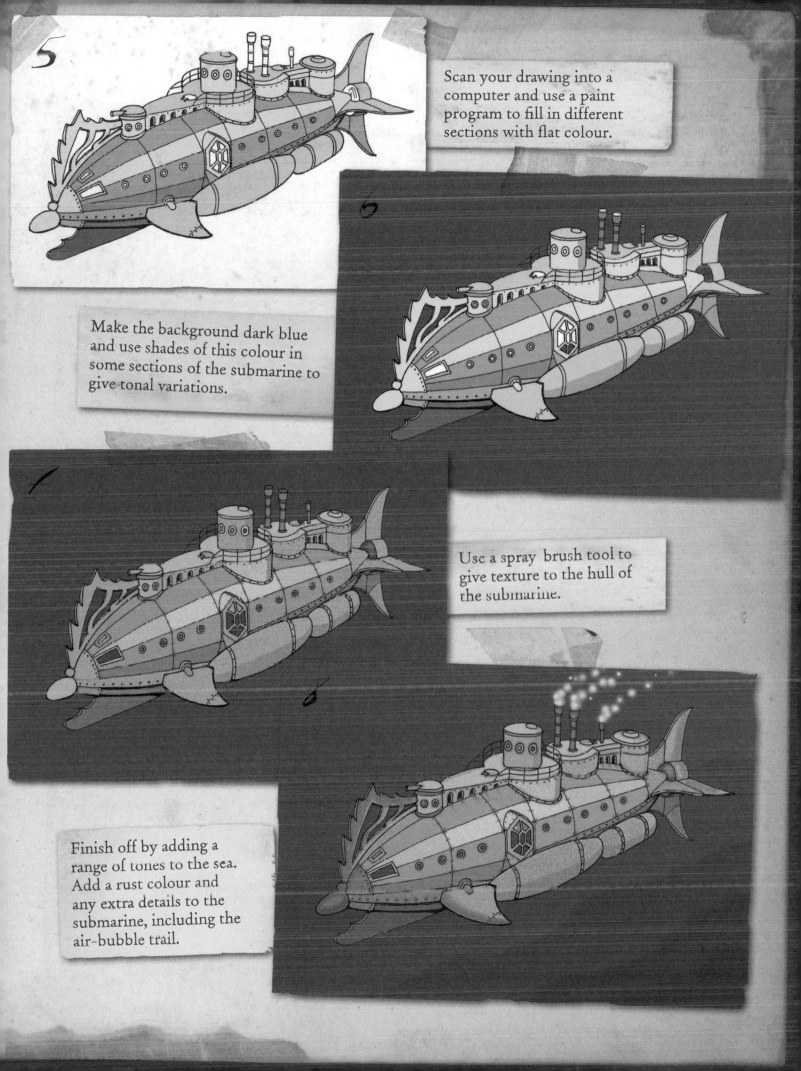

5

Scan your drawing into a computer and use a paint program to fill in different sections with flat colour.

6

Make the background dark blue and use shades of this colour in some sections of the submarine to give tonal variations.

7

Use a spray brush tool to give texture to the hull of the submarine.

8

Finish off by adding a range of tones to the sea. Add a rust colour and any extra details to the submarine, including the air-bubble trail.

GLOSSARY

Chiaroscuro   The use of light and dark in a drawing.

Cross-hatching   A series of criss-crossing lines used to add dark shading to a drawing.

Hatching   A series of parallel lines used to add medium shading to a drawing.

Three-dimensional   Having an effect of depth, so as to look lifelike or real.

Vanishing point   The place in a perspective drawing where parallel lines appear to meet.

INDEX